Meeting
Jesus

6 GROUP BIBLE STUDIES FOR LENT

Elizabeth Rundle

Published 2007 by CWR, Waverley Abbey House, Waverley Lane, Farnham, Surrey GU9 8EP, UK. Registered Charity No. 294387. Registered Limited Company No. 1990308.

Unless otherwise indicated, all Scripture references are from the Holy Bible: New International Version (NIV), copyright © 1973, 1978, 1984 by the International Bible Society.

Other versions are marked:

Message: Scripture taken from *The Message*. Copyright © 1993, 1994, 1995, 1996, 2000, 2001, 2002. Used by permission of NavPress Publishing Group.

Concept development, editing, design and production by CWR
Cover image: Design Pics Inc.

Printed in Croatia by Zrinski

ISBN: 978-1-85345-442-4

Contents

Contents

Introduction

Lent may be one of the few times in the year when people take time to pause regularly to study God's Word, often in organised Lent groups.

Of course, the Bible is read each week in church services of all denominations, but within a service format there is seldom opportunity to ask questions or to put the snippet of Scripture into context. Then the routine of life takes over and those questions that flitted across our minds are quickly buried under the responsibilities of our daily routines.

Someone who had been a regular church-goer all her life asked: 'Did Jesus go into the wilderness at the beginning of Holy Week?' This is an understandable assumption when we recognise that Jesus' temptations in the wilderness are traditionally recounted at the beginning of Lent. Strangely, we don't seem to hear the story at any other time of the year. Biblical events get lumped together in our minds, compartmentalised to the extent that we miss the overall picture. The Person of Jesus becomes distorted if we do not take enough time to trace His life, miracles and teaching as the Gospel writers intended.

I am reminded of a modern parable in which a couple visited a stately home. When they arrived they made straight for the restaurant and had a good meal. After their meal they decided to go into the delightfully scented shop, and the time just flew! By the time they had looked at everything in the shop there wasn't really enough time to go into the house itself, so they went and sat by the lake. They bought ice creams and marvelled at how many cars and coaches had crammed the car park and how lovely the flowers looked. The next day they told everyone what a good time they'd had and how they had enjoyed the stately home.

However, the fact remained that although the couple had passed the great front door, they had not actually gone inside the stately home. They had not seen the priceless works of art, the gifts from around the world, the exquisite craftsmanship in the antique furniture and the personal mementos that gave the house its identity. They had not appreciated the hundreds of people whose labour had brought the great house into being from the architect's first design on paper. That stately home was the embodiment of brilliant human gifts, achievements, sweat, toil and generosity, and the history of generations.

The visiting couple had glimpsed the outside but had not experienced the fascinating interior for themselves.

Many people behave in just the same way with the Bible. It contains such treasures, such breath-taking promises and words of comfort. It is also the product of many 'hands', borne out of personal experience of the saving love of God at various moments in history. It contains stories of great achievements and titanic disasters, people of outstanding faith and virtue and, more often, ordinary, doubting, troubled men and women who longed to know peace and justice.

In Ephesians 3:17–18 the apostle Paul wrote:

> And I pray that you, being rooted and established in love, may have power, together with all the saints, to grasp how wide and long and high and deep is the love of Christ, and to know this love that surpasses knowledge – that you may be filled to the measure of all the fullness of God.

We cannot be 'rooted' or 'established' if we remain on the fringe. My prayer is that during this Lent study, we, like the characters we focus on, will meet with Jesus and find inspiration to be forever grounded in 'the love of Christ'.

It was this love that took Him to the cross for the sins of the world – your sins and mine.

As I have worked on this Lent study, four distinct aims have been laid on my heart.

Firstly, that as disciples, our first priority is to meet with the living Lord Jesus and to acknowledge His touch on our lives today. We need to recognise that He is the Son of God – the Messiah – whose life, death and resurrection was, and is, world transforming. We must also recognise, however, that at the same time, in mystery and miracle, Jesus is the Lord of the individual – our *personal* Lord and Saviour.

Secondly, in these six sessions, I would like us to explore how meeting Jesus changed the lives of seven very different people. These people's homes, families and friends were all affected by the impact Jesus made on their lives. The Gospels don't record fairy tales in 'never-never land' but deliver to us the memory of real people in real places with real needs; needs which echo through each generation. As Peter wrote: 'We did not follow cleverly invented stories when we told you about the power and coming of our Lord Jesus Christ, but we were eye-witnesses of his majesty' (2 Pet. 1:16).

Thirdly, I want us to see that these people we study – Jairus' daughter, the rich young ruler, Lazarus, the woman bent double, Bartimaeus and the Pharisees, Nicodemus and Joseph of Arimathea – were among the first ever 'living stones' of the embryonic Christian community. It was from their witness and testimony, as well as the disciples', that others were brought into the knowledge and love of Jesus Christ. It was out of their struggles and disappointments, joys and prayers that the new communities of faith began to grow.

The disciples may have been given the 'great commission', as recorded at the end of Matthew's Gospel, to 'go and make disciples of all nations', but our seven characters were ones who witnessed 'at home'. And, sometimes, 'home' can be the hardest place of all to proclaim the power and love of Jesus Christ.

Apart from Nicodemus and Joseph of Arimathea, there is no record of the other individuals being in Jerusalem during the period of Jesus' last week before His crucifixion. But, we do know that all devout Jews would make the annual pilgrimage for the Passover celebrations if they possibly could. So, I have used the 'Imagine' sections in these studies purely to root the events at the close of our Lord's earthly life in the sequence they occurred and to enable us to engage with the rising religious and political tensions in Jerusalem. There is also the opportunity to imagine how we would feel to be caught up in the unfolding drama as the 'crowd' opinion descended from adulation to condemnation.

Then, fourthly, I hope that as you work through this study, you will feel drawn beyond the pages you are reading to learn more and more of your Saviour Jesus and to take your part as His disciple today. His words and His love are not fossilised remains from two thousand years ago, they are *living words* and *everlasting love* offered to you and to all the world in every time and place.

Jesus Christ is the same yesterday and today and for ever. Hebrews 13:8

I would like to offer you a 'Lent Challenge'. Each day, from the beginning of Lent (Ash Wednesday) could you read one whole chapter of Matthew's Gospel? Then save chapter 28 until Easter Day. You will be amazed at how God will speak to you through the reading of His Word as you make your own spiritual journey to Jerusalem.

As you prepare for these studies, be encouraged by the words of Peter – fisherman, disciple and evangelist:

> Grace and peace be yours in abundance through the knowledge of God and of Jesus our Lord.
> 2 Peter 1:2

Jairus' Daughter

Icebreaker

If members of the group do not know each other, take a few minutes at the beginning of this first session to introduce yourselves, starting with the leader. With these initial formalities over, briefly discuss which famous personality – past or present – you would most like to meet.

Worship Focus

Each week, create a linking Worship Focus. For the opening session, place a cross (it doesn't have to be big but it would be best if it were free-standing) on a material-covered table or box. The material could be purple, as this is the colour associated with Lent. At the foot of the cross place an open Bible and a child's toy.

Consider these objects as you move into the next part of the study.

Opening Prayer

Come to us, Lord Jesus Christ. By the power of Your Spirit, open our eyes, open our minds and open our hearts to the miracle of Your loving presence. As we pray and search Your Holy Word together, deepen our faith in an atmosphere of encouragement and trust. Meet with us, Lord Jesus Christ. Bless us in the coming weeks, that we may grow in grace, to the glory of Your name. Amen.

First Bible Reading
Luke 8:40–42,49–55

Now when Jesus returned, a crowd welcomed him, for they were all expecting him. Then a man named Jairus, a ruler of the synagogue, came and fell at Jesus' feet, pleading with him to come to his house because his only daughter, a girl of about twelve, was dying …

While Jesus was still speaking, someone came from the house of Jairus, the synagogue ruler. 'Your daughter is dead,' he said. 'Don't bother the teacher any more.'

Hearing this, Jesus said to Jairus, 'Don't be afraid; just believe, and she will be healed.'

When he arrived at the house of Jairus, he did not let anyone go in with him except Peter, John and James, and the child's father and mother. Meanwhile, all the people were wailing and mourning for her. 'Stop wailing,' Jesus said. 'She is not dead but asleep.'

They laughed at him, knowing that she was dead. But he took her by the hand and said, 'My child, get up!' Her spirit returned, and at once she stood up. Then Jesus told them to give her something to eat.

Setting the Scene

The Capernaum Jesus would have known was a bustling market village with little houses built in the local black basalt stone. Smells from the fresh, drying and salting fish mingled with those of the market stalls selling spices and vegetables. This food fed the local population as well as the Roman garrison. The people co-existed with the occupying soldiers far better in Galilee than in Jerusalem, a point underlined by the unusual fact that one of the centurions had built the local synagogue (Luke 7:1–5).

Due to its position at the northern end of the Sea of Galilee, Capernaum had grown into the commercial hub for the surrounding villages. (It is easier for us today, with our ever-rising population, to consider what Gospel authors called a 'town', a 'village' and what they called a 'city', a 'town'.) Merchants from Damascus would be seen with silks and other gorgeous fabrics, haggling with merchants from the Mediterranean coast; camel trains and mules added to the general noise – and odour.

When we recall that there were ten 'cities' around this area in Galilee – the Decapolis – it causes us to wonder why Matthew, Mark, Luke and John did not mention them when

recording Jesus' preaching, teaching and healing ministry. Scholars estimate that each of those 'cities' had populations of between 10,000 and 15,000, but in New Testament terms they didn't exist. Why? Our answer lies in their being 'foreign'; a humiliating reminder of Gentile occupation; the Greeks and latterly the Romans. Capernaum, however, was a village for indigenous Galileans.

Matthew tells us: 'Leaving Nazareth, he went and lived in Capernaum ...' (4:13). Jesus made Capernaum the base for His ministry. It was also the home of the fishermen disciples – the brothers Simon Peter and Andrew, James and John – the home of Philip and the tax collector and Matthew. In Capernaum, Jesus was among friends, and without the undercurrents and tensions of Jerusalem. He taught regularly in the synagogue, which was a stone's throw from the Sea of Galilee. As Matthew, Mark and Luke all mention Jairus by name, and given his position as ruler of the synagogue, we may reasonably deduce that Jesus and Jairus knew each other well. In the expected hospitality of those days, it is more than likely Jesus would have eaten in Jairus' home.

Session Focus

Recent newspapers have carried heart-rending stories of families seeking the best possible quality of life for their children living with severe physical and mental limitations. Two families in particular have been highlighted, one on either side of the Atlantic. Their daily problems appear insurmountable, the prognosis for the future dismal – but they keep going. They have to. Such is the bond between parent and child that parents will go to the uttermost limits for their beloved and vulnerable child. This is God-implanted instinct.

When we hear the story of Jairus and his daughter, especially those of us who are parents, we can feel an instant sympathy with this father. In the face of disaster he desperately clutched at any straw to avoid facing what everyone else saw as obvious: his little girl was dead.

Jairus had position and influence in Capernaum; many people would have envied his comfortable lifestyle. Personally and professionally, Jairus' life was good. Then suddenly, everything changed.

Remember that if the little girl had been dead, contact with her would have made both Jairus and Jesus unclean. However, for those who have not seen a dead person before, and depending on the nature of the illness, it isn't always easy to know the precise moment of death. Jairus could not believe what was happening to his daughter and the only person he could think of to help was Jesus.

I believe that at one time or another, we all reach these kind of moments. Moments of blind panic, when we ask: Where is God?

Let's look at how Luke projects Jesus in this chapter. Jesus proves His power over creation (8:22–25); He proves His power over things we do not understand (vv.26–39) and then His sovereign power over sickness and health, life and death.

This is the power of God.

Luke's staggering claims about Jesus are wrapped in simple, short stories that have been told and retold over twenty centuries. As we use this Lent study, let us take the precious extra time we have set apart to draw closer to God, and prayerfully study the meaning and the implications of this story on our lives today.

Jairus' daughter being brought back from the brink of burial is a story with a happy ending. However, experience of life teaches us that Christianity is not a cocoon against tragedy, and a reliance on the Living Presence does not mean that we should expect miracles to be conjured up for our benefit. Rather, it moves us to seek the Son of God who suffered and died for the sins of all time, and who suffers now within each individual stricken heart. Through witnessed suffering, our hearts are made to pause and think. In the touch of people's kindness, skill and prayer, there is a strength, a hope and a love beyond our human understanding. God holds us even when we have given up.

Interlude

Song: 'Hosanna, hosanna, hosanna to the King of kings' by Carl Tuttle
Song: 'How lovely on the mountains' by Leonard E. Smith
Song: 'Children of Jerusalem' by John Henley
'Rejoice greatly, O daughter of Zion' from Messiah by Handel

Second Bible Reading
John 12:12–19

The next day the great crowd that had come for the Feast heard that Jesus was on his way to Jerusalem. They took palm branches and went out to meet him, shouting,

'Hosanna!'

'Blessed is he who comes in the name of the Lord!'

'Blessed is the King of Israel!'

Jesus found a young donkey and sat upon it, as it is written,

'Do not be afraid, O Daughter of Zion;
  see, your king is coming,
  seated on a donkey's colt.'

At first his disciples did not understand all this. Only

after Jesus was glorified did they realise that these things had been written about him and that they had done these things to him.

Now the crowd that was with him when he called Lazarus from the tomb and raised him from the dead continued to spread the word. Many people, because they had heard that he had given this miraculous sign, went out to meet him. So the Pharisees said one to another, 'See, this is getting us nowhere. Look how the whole world has gone after him!'

Imagine

The commemoration of Passover is the oldest continually celebrated religious festival in the world. We are told by the Gospel writer, Luke, that Mary and Joseph took Jesus to Jerusalem every year for the Feast of the Passover (Luke 2:41). This was quite an undertaking for people from Nazareth because it would mean a walk of some seventy to eighty miles, but it emphasises for us the importance of Passover. Clearly, Jesus continued this observance throughout His adult life. Although we annually celebrate the Easter story, there is still nothing with which we can compare in our own Christian calendar to this annual pilgrimage and re-enactment of the Passover meal.

Why should Luke be so specific about Jairus' daughter being twelve years old? It may have been because she had reached the age of recognised womanhood. As Jairus was a ruler of the synagogue in Capernaum, his daughter would probably have joined her parents and other family members on their pilgrimage to Jerusalem.

Just imagine that Jairus' daughter had gone to Jerusalem that fateful year of Jesus' crucifixion. How excited she would have been to see her hero, Jesus, riding into the Holy City amidst the crowds shouting 'Hosanna!'. Imagine how heartily Jairus would have joined in, waving his palm

branch and shouting for the Teacher who had given him back his daughter.

Now imagine how you would feel to meet a person who had saved your life. I expect you would be their greatest admirer and supporter. Would you feel proud to count that person as your friend? Would you be enthusiastic in your public testimony about what that person had done for you? Would you want to follow his or her career? Perhaps this gives you a flavour of the joy and expectation surrounding Jesus as He made His sensational entry into the city. But also, hold in your mind that even at such a time of jubilation there was a deadly undercurrent of anger and hate as certain men plotted His murder.

Discussion Starters

1. What healing miracles can you think of which Jairus may have witnessed?

_____

_____

_____

_____

2. Who might that 'someone' have been who came to tell Jairus his daughter was dead?

_____

_____

_____

_____

3. Why is it good for our mental and physical health to weep and mourn rather than bottle our feelings up?

_____

_____

_____

_____

4. How does it affect your faith when you see a child suffering and prayers for healing not answered in the way you want?

_____

_____

_____

_____

5. Are you able to share with the group a time when you have pleaded with God? Or, has someone ever saved your life?

_____

_____

_____

_____

6. 'Every life, however short, is a miracle and a gift from God.' Discuss.

_____

_____

_____

_____

7. How would you describe the significance of Jesus entering Jerusalem on a donkey to a person of another faith?

_____

_____

_____

_____

8. Children needlessly die because of contaminated water. Suggest ways in which we can respond to God's loving sacrifice in Jesus Christ and help 'save' the life of a child somewhere.

_____

_____

_____

_____

Final Thoughts

Our thinking and discussions may lead us to deeper gratitude for what we have – to a greater appreciation of the people who make up our family, workplace and community. Tragedies break in on our lives and we are shaken by our own vulnerability. We may ask the human questions, 'What am I here for?' or 'How could this happen?' The miracle of Jairus' daughter being brought back to life is so much more than a story with a happy ending; it is affirmation that Jesus was the human face of God the Giver of Life. Jesus was and is 'Immanuel', meaning 'God with us!' 'Hosanna' means 'Lord, save us'. And Jesus has saved us. He has saved our lives by His death on the cross.

Closing Prayer

LEADER: God of grace and holiness,
Forgive us that so often we enjoy Gospel stories rather

than letting the words challenge and encourage us to discipleship. In these moments we commit to Your eternal keeping those known to us who face their own personal tragedies today. *(Pause)*

We praise You for the miracle of life and the promise of *everlasting* life in and through our Lord and Saviour, Jesus Christ. At all times and in all places may we feel the peace of Your presence.

ALL: Amen.

Further Study

Psalms 117; 118:25–29. Psalm 122, which would have been a psalm Jesus and all pilgrims would have recited as they approached Jerusalem. Revelation 21:1–4.

A Rich Young Man

Icebreaker

Think of your most prized possession. How did you acquire it, and how would you feel if you had to part with it?

Worship Focus

On the material-covered table, place the cross. Then place a Bible open at Psalm 119 on the table and, finally, place a leather or material purse at the foot of the cross with silver coins spilling from it.

Opening Prayer

(Adapted from King David's Prayer in 1 Chronicles 29:10–13.)

We praise You, O Lord, God and Father of Your people from everlasting to everlasting.

Yours, O Lord is the greatness and the power, and the glory and the majesty and the splendour. Everything in heaven and earth is Yours.

Wealth and honour come from You. You are ruler of all things.

Now, our God, we give You thanks, and praise Your glorious name in and through our Lord and Saviour Jesus Christ. Amen.

First Bible Reading

Luke 18:18–23

A certain ruler asked him, 'Good teacher, what must I do to inherit eternal life?'

'Why do you call me good?' Jesus answered. 'No-one is good – except God alone. You know the commandments: 'Do not commit adultery, do not murder, do not steal, do not give false testimony, honour your father and mother.'

'All these I have kept since I was a boy,' he said.

When Jesus heard this, he said to him, 'You still lack one thing. Sell everything you have and give to the poor, and you will have treasure in heaven. Then come, follow me.'

When he heard this, he became very sad, because he was a man of great wealth.

Setting the Scene

Jesus had left Galilee and was on His journey to Jerusalem. He took the 'scenic route' through Samaria and then down across the River Jordan into the region of Perea. This was close to where John the Baptist had taught huge crowds and baptised people. Jesus had also been baptised there by John before He started His public ministry. It seems that it was just as Jesus and the disciples were leaving Perea on their way to Jericho that the ruler made his approach.

Luke calls him 'a certain ruler', Matthew calls him a man 'with great wealth' and Mark records how he 'ran up to' Jesus and 'fell on his knees' in reverence before Him. From these three accounts we piece together a picture of a young man, with, as we might say, the world at his feet, rushing to catch Jesus before He left town. He abased himself at Jesus' feet and blurted out the question that had been gnawing away at his conscience since he had first listened to His teaching.

Perhaps he had heard Jesus tell the parable of the Pharisee and the tax collector, a parable that had burst his self-satisfied bubble. Or he may have been watching as Jesus put his arms around the children. Either way, he had certainly seen and heard enough about Jesus to consider Him worthy of the highest respect. What is certain is that the young ruler, rich though he may have been, was obviously in awe of the travelling rabbi, and maybe that's why he only plucked up the courage to approach Jesus at the last minute.

With all the idealism of youth and the confidence that wealth and authority bestow, he waited for Jesus to solve

his dilemma and give him the key to spiritual success. No doubt the disciples and all the other people around Jesus were also waiting to hear how He would answer.

Session Focus

This young man appears to be every mother's dream – ever since he was a boy he had kept *all* the commandments! He was eager, in the full vigour of early manhood, respectable, reliable, rich … he had everything. Well, almost everything. This fine young ruler was honest enough to realise that deep down something was missing.

The leader should now pick up the Bible from the table and read Psalm 119:9–14. As a religious boy, this was one of the psalms which the young ruler would have been able to recite:

> How can a young man keep his way pure?
>> By living according to your word.
> I seek you with all my heart;
>> do not let me stray from your commands.
> I have hidden your word in my heart
>> that I might not sin against you.
> Praise be to you, O LORD;
>> teach me your decrees.
> With my lips I recount
>> all the laws that come from your mouth.
> I rejoice in following your statutes
>> as one rejoices in great riches.

All his life the young man had done the right thing and, in meeting Jesus, he was making the most important connection of his life. His only mistake lay in his expectation that he himself could 'do' something in his own power to inherit eternal life. And even if we think our attitudes are different to his in the light of the New Testament, I have a sneaking suspicion that we all have a tendency of trying to accrue brownie points to justify ourselves before other people … and before God.

Many people are concerned by Jesus' answer to the young man and argue that it is impractical and irresponsible to give away all your resources. There is a strong and plausible argument that the weak can only be helped by those who remain strong. However, let's put it another way. Jesus knew the young man's wealth had become a barrier between himself and God. Although he genuinely thought that he had kept all the commandments, without realising it, the man's wealth had made him break the first commandment of all: 'You shall have no other gods before me' (Exod. 20:3). Jesus was asking this young ruler to put God first in his life and only then, in denying himself, could he know God's priceless gift of eternal life.

Mark's Gospel says: 'Jesus looked at him and loved him' (10:21). What a sincere disciple he would have made, what a pillar of the Early Church he could have become. But Mark also records the young man's response: 'he went away sad.' Some translations say 'he was shocked'. Giving up everything he had known, his security and status … it was too much. He wanted eternal life – but not enough. At that crucial moment in his young life, on his knees before Jesus, discipleship posed too high a cost.

When the period of Lent arrives, many people feel they are doing 'the right thing' by giving up something: chocolate or wine or some other frivolous indulgence. It may be an uncomfortable question to ask, but why do we give up trivialities rather than respond to the voice of Jesus which says, 'Follow me'?

Following Jesus involves a greater cost than giving up chocolate.

Meeting Jesus challenged the rich young man's lifestyle to its core. I would like to feel that he went home and did some hard thinking. And perhaps, in this special period of Lent, Jesus is waiting for us to do the same.

Interlude

Song: 'I'd rather have Jesus' by R.F. Miller
Song: 'I, the Lord of sea and sky (Here I am, Lord)' by Daniel L. Schutte
Hymn: 'O for a closer walk with God' by William Cowper
'Money, Money, Money' by Abba

Second Bible Reading
John 13:2,21–30

The evening meal was being served, and the devil had already prompted Judas Iscariot, son of Simon, to betray Jesus …

Jesus was troubled in spirit and testified, 'I tell you the truth, one of you is going to betray me.'

His disciples stared at one another … One of them, the disciple whom Jesus loved, was reclining next to him. Simon Peter motioned to this disciple and said, 'Ask him which one he means.'

Leaning back against Jesus, he asked him, 'Lord, who is it?'

Jesus answered, 'It is the one to whom I will give this piece of bread when I have dipped it in the dish.' Then, dipping the piece of bread, he gave it to Judas Iscariot, son of Simon. As soon as Judas took the bread, Satan entered into him.

'What you are about to do, do quickly,' Jesus told him, but no-one at the meal understood why Jesus said this to him. Since Judas had charge of the money, some thought Jesus was telling him to buy what was needed for the Feast, or to give something to the poor. As soon as Judas had taken the bread, he went out. And it was night.

Imagine

Our second Bible reading also features a faithfully religious man, this time one of Jesus' own twelve disciples, Judas Iscariot, son of Simon. Judas was so trusted by everyone that he was the group's 'treasurer' and was above suspicion. No one thought anything of his leaving the meal table.

The Bible only mentions three people specifically as people whom Jesus loved: the rich young ruler, Lazarus and, we assume it to be, the disciple John. We can only infer from this that as well as John, the other two were also significant people in the ministry of Jesus and also in the life of the Early Church.

So, imagine for a moment you are watching Judas slip out into the cold night. What symbolism! He deliberately chose to leave warm companionship and go into the cold dark of betrayal. (You will find the record of Judas going to the chief priests and officers of the Temple guard in Matthew 26:14–16 and Luke 22:1–6.) He was willing to sell his Lord and Master for thirty pieces of silver; the Lord who, only hours before, had lovingly washed his feet.

There is a cynical phrase which says, 'every man has his price', but did Judas really need the money he received for betraying Jesus? Imagine the contempt the chief priests had for Judas.

Now imagine how you would feel if someone sold your secrets, betrayed your trust and made money out of you. Could you forgive them?

Discussion Starters

1. Which commandments might we break without realising, and how?

   _____

   _____

   _____

   _____

2. Which do you consider to be the hardest commandment to keep?

   _____

   _____

   _____

   _____

3. Suppose your neighbour came and asked you what he or she should do to inherit eternal life – what would you say?

   _____

   _____

   _____

   _____

4. If you had one million pounds to give away, what would you do with it?

   _____

   _____

   _____

   _____

5. Discuss the discipline of tithing – giving one tenth of your income for God's work. If it is such a good idea, why doesn't everyone do it?

_____

_____

_____

_____

6. Judas had his reason(s) for betraying his Master for thirty pieces of silver. Discuss in your group what you think those reasons might have been.

_____

_____

_____

_____

7. Twice the Gospel writer John mentions the name of Judas' father. This indicates that Simon was known to the early Christians. Consider the effect Judas' betrayal and his subsequent suicide had on his family.

_____

_____

_____

_____

8. Jesus knew what Judas intended. He knew Peter would disown Him. Jesus knows all about each one of us and yet is still willing to forgive us our sins. Share with each other how this makes you feel.

_____

_____

_____

_____

Final Thoughts

Respectability and a decent lifestyle are not sufficient qualifications for becoming a follower of Jesus Christ. Some of the richest and most beautiful people in the world have proved to be far from content, so, in your personal prayer time, ask yourself what your prized possession is. Consider how you are following Jesus – do possessions mean so much that they have become a barrier to your discipleship; where in your life is there room to serve with love without being paid?

Take time to evaluate how this period of Lent can prepare you for better stewardship of your resources and for greater commitment to the teaching of our Lord.

Closing Prayer

LEADER: Let us pray using words of a hymn by Frances Ridley Havergal[1]:
ALL: Take my silver and my gold,
not a mite would I withhold;
Take my intellect, and use
Every power as Thou shalt choose.
Take my love; my Lord, I pour
At Thy feet its treasure store;
Take myself, and I will be
ever, only, all for Thee.
(Allow some moments of silence for personal reflection.)

LEADER: Loving heavenly Father, we commit all that we have and are to be used to spread the gospel of justice, peace and co-operation. Send us out in the power of Your Holy Spirit, to live and work to the praise and glory of Jesus Christ.
ALL: Thanks be to God. Amen.

Further Study

Luke 4:1–13; 16:19–31; John 13:34–35.

Note

1. Frances Ridley Havergal, 'Take My Life', 1874.

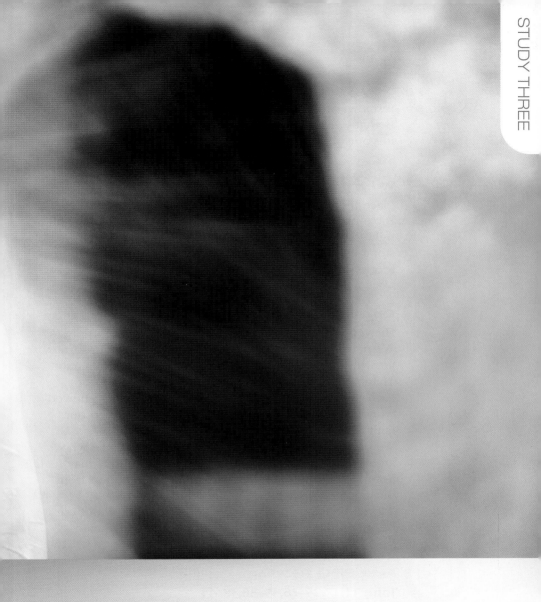

Lazarus

Icebreaker

Jesus was a welcome guest in Lazarus' home in Bethany. How would you make Jesus feel 'at home' in your house today?

Worship Focus

Place the cross in the centre of the table with an open Bible on the left and a small posy-shaped wreath on the right. Each member of the group should be given a small stone or pebble and be invited to place the pebble at the foot of the cross in memory of a loved one.

Opening Prayer

Heavenly Father, we praise You for the gift of this day. We praise You for the changing seasons, for signs of new growth, new life and new hope we see in Your creation. Thank You for the gift of our lives, and we pray for each person here today. Fill us with new hope, renewed wonder and reawakened joy that we may deepen our faith together as we study Your Word.

We bring before You our friends, especially those who are ill, in body, mind or spirit. We pray that they may feel Your strength in their weakness, and take comfort from our prayers.

We ask this spoken prayer and the silent prayers of our hearts, in the name of Jesus Christ the Healer. Amen.

First Bible Reading
John 11:17,25–26,35–36,38–44

On his arrival, Jesus found Lazarus had already been in the tomb for four days …

Jesus said to [Martha], 'I am the resurrection and the life. He who believes in me will live, even though he dies; and whoever lives and believes in me will never die' …

Jesus wept.

Then the Jews said, 'See how he loved him!' …

Jesus, once more deeply moved, came to the tomb. It was a cave with a stone laid across the entrance. 'Take away the stone,' he said.

'But, Lord,' said Martha, the sister of the dead man, 'by this time there is a bad odour, for he has been there four days.'

Then Jesus said, 'Did I not tell you that if you believed, you would see the glory of God?'

So they took away the stone. Then Jesus looked up and said, 'Father, I thank you that you have heard me. I knew that you always hear me, but I said this for the benefit of the people standing here, that they may believe that you sent me.'

When he had said this, Jesus called in a loud voice, 'Lazarus, come out!' The dead man came out, his hands and feet wrapped with strips of linen, and a cloth around his face.

Jesus said to them, 'Take off the grave clothes and let him go.'

Setting the Scene

Archaeologists have found ossuaries in Bethany with Galilean inscriptions. These ossuaries – small boxes which housed the bones of loved ones – shed new light on the inhabitants of Bethany, a village so far away from Galilee. It seems that several Galilean families had moved south to the area around Jerusalem and, over the years, many had gravitated to Bethany. Today's shifting population is nothing new! Maybe that was why Jesus felt so much at home with Martha, Mary and Lazarus. They may even have shared mutual friends and family.

In any event, Jesus and the disciples appear to have been regular visitors to Lazarus' home. When the sisters realised

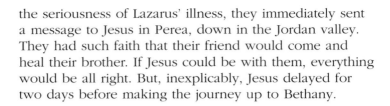

the seriousness of Lazarus' illness, they immediately sent a message to Jesus in Perea, down in the Jordan valley. They had such faith that their friend would come and heal their brother. If Jesus could be with them, everything would be all right. But, inexplicably, Jesus delayed for two days before making the journey up to Bethany.

On a previous visit to Jerusalem, Jesus had healed the sick at the pool of Bethesda and in subsequent teaching had revealed: 'For just as the Father raises the dead and gives them life, even so the Son gives life to whom he is pleased to give it ... I tell you the truth, whoever hears my word and believes him who sent me has eternal life ...' (John 5:21,24). The scene is set for the last recorded miracle in John's Gospel. The last and the greatest. Jesus proves His divine, God-appointed power over life and death.

However, this miracle in Bethany so enraged the chief priests and Pharisees that they summoned a meeting of the Sanhedrin, their traditional religious court.

John describes how the members of the Sanhedrin feared that Jesus' unrivalled popularity would cause the Romans to remove their authority and even threaten their nation with another exile (John 11:48). Such was the heightened tension that it was no longer safe for Jesus to move freely, and 'Therefore Jesus no longer moved about publicly among the Jews' (John 11:54). Not only Jesus, but Lazarus was also in fear of his life: 'So the chief priests made plans to kill Lazarus as well ...' (12:10).

Session Focus

Christianity is a resurrection faith, yet the spiritual concept of resurrection lies in the ancient writings of the great Moses, who, at the close of his long life stated: '... I have set before you life and death, blessings and curses. Now choose life, so that you and your children may live and

that you may love the LORD your God … For the LORD
is your life …' (Deut. 30:19–20). But Jesus makes the
astonishing claim: 'I am the resurrection and the life.'

Jesus takes upon Himself what has been the sole
authority of God. No wonder C.S. Lewis said Jesus was
one of three things: the most blasphemous of all con-
men, completely mad or, as He claimed, the Son of God.
There are no other options.

The Sadducees, the aristocracy of the priesthood,
denied any form of resurrection, but the Pharisees did
hold to this belief. It would appear by Martha's reply
to Jesus' statement that many of the people believed in
resurrection, even if they had no idea of what it really
meant. The Old Testament writers offered glimpses of this
hope. The book of Job holds enigmatic verses: 'I know
that my Redeemer lives, and that in the end he will stand
upon the earth. And after my skin has been destroyed,
yet in my flesh I will see God …' (Job 19:25–26). And the
prophet Isaiah was inspired to write: 'But your dead will
live; their bodies will rise. You who dwell in the dust,
wake up and shout for joy' (Isa. 26:19). These thought
strands, married with the mysterious writings of Daniel –
'Multitudes who sleep in the dust of the earth will awake:
some to everlasting life …' (Dan. 12:2) – created belief in
some form of resurrection. In bringing Lazarus back to life
after four days (when it was commonly accepted that the
soul had left the body and death was final), Jesus injected
a new dimension to the debate. He showed that:

- with God, all things are possible
- belief in Him is the key.

There are two particular cantatas associated with the
events of Holy Week that I love. One is *Olivet to Calvary*
and the other is *Crucifixion*. In the latter work, by John
Stainer, John 3:16 is set to music beautifully: 'God so

loved the world that he gave his only begotten son, that whoso [sic] believeth in him, should not perish but have everlasting life.' We hear the echo of these words when Jesus responded to Martha in our first reading, when she told her Lord that her brother Lazarus was dead. The Greek word for 'perish' holds a much wider meaning than just 'death'; it also infers 'waste' or 'write off'. What encouragement from Jesus. It's never a waste to believe and trust in Him; our lives will never be written off. It's beyond our human minds to understand, but not beyond our human hearts to believe.

Interlude
'God so loved the world' from *Crucifixion* by Stainer or Song: 'I am the bread of life' (with the chorus 'And I will raise him up') by S. Suzanne Toolan
Part of the *Andante* from Bruch's violin concerto

Second Bible Reading
Mark 14:43–50
Just as Jesus was speaking, Judas, one of the Twelve, appeared. With him was a crowd armed with swords and clubs, sent from the chief priests, the teachers of the law, and the elders.

Now the betrayer had arranged a signal with them: 'The one I kiss is the man; arrest him and lead him away under guard.' Going at once to Jesus, Judas said, 'Rabbi!' and kissed him. The men seized Jesus and arrested him. Then one of those standing near drew his sword and struck the servant of the high priest, cutting off his ear.

'Am I leading a rebellion,' said Jesus, 'that you have come out with swords and clubs to capture me? Every day I was with you, teaching in the temple courts, and you did not arrest me. But the Scriptures must be ful-filled.' Then everyone deserted him and fled.

Imagine

Look at the last sentence of our second Bible reading again: 'Then everyone deserted him …'

Is there anything more psychologically cruel than to be abandoned? The disciples had been Jesus' closest friends, and now they had all gone. Perhaps we are so used to hearing this story that the tragic impact has become diluted to the point where we lose our capacity to connect with the atmosphere of Jerusalem 2,000 years ago.

The Garden of Gethsemane was roughly mid-way between Bethany and Jerusalem. Imagine Lazarus keeping a low profile and not leaving the village, but hearing the rumours coming from Jerusalem and becoming increasingly agitated. Jesus, his deliverer and his friend, the rabbi to whom he owed his life, was in mortal danger.

Imagine Lazarus, his concern for Jesus now outweighing fears for his own safety, creeping over to the Mount of Olives under cover of darkness. Everyone knew Jesus and the disciples regularly rested and prayed in the Garden of Gethsemane – he needed to warn them of the mounting danger. Imagine how Lazarus would have felt when he realised he was too late. He watched the mob closing in on Jesus with clubs and swords! Ah, but Judas was with them so there was nothing to … suddenly, Jesus was arrested! How could Judas betray his Master? Lazarus fled back to Bethany to keep his sisters safe.

Now imagine your own emotions if you had seen Jesus arrested. Take a time-leap and 'see' Judas coming over to kiss Jesus. 'See' the gentle Son of God roughly manhandled out of the peaceful garden. 'Look' for the disciples, for anyone to speak for Jesus, for anyone to stand by Him … there's no one. After all the skirmish, noise and blood, the olive grove is dark and silent.

Discussion Starters

1. Martha and Mary felt things would have been different if Jesus had been with them. Who is the person you would rely on in a crisis?

   _____

   _____

   _____

   _____

2. Elisha raised the Shunamite woman's son (2 Kings 4:32–37) but Jesus raised three people – Jairus' daughter, the widow of Nain's son (Luke 7:11–17) and Lazarus. What does this say to us about the Person and purpose of Jesus?

   _____

   _____

   _____

   _____

3. Modern advances in medical science enable people to recover from illnesses which would have caused their death in previous generations. In what ways can we show our gratitude for the 'extra' years of life?

   _____

   _____

   _____

   _____

4. Without embarrassing elaboration, perhaps with just
a simple 'yes' or 'no', can you say if there has been a
time when you have left someone but later wished you
had stayed with them?

_____

_____

_____

_____

5. How would you explain the meaning of eternal life?

_____

_____

_____

_____

6. Discuss how you would feel to see Jesus arrested?

_____

_____

_____

_____

7. How would you expect Judas to be treated after his
betrayal?

_____

_____

_____

_____

8. Jesus chose Gethsemane as a quiet place to pray. Where would you choose to go to struggle in prayer, and why?

_____

_____

_____

_____

Final Thoughts

The raising of Lazarus is an obvious precursor to God raising Jesus from the dead. To say that we can understand resurrection completely would be arrogance and quite untrue. However, think of faith as a giant jigsaw. We struggle with a bit here and a couple of bits there, and many times feel that we are never going to be able to grasp the whole picture. But we are not alone in feeling like this; look at what Paul wrote in 1 Corinthians 13:12: 'We don't yet see things clearly. We're squinting in a fog, peering through a mist' (*Message*). Take heart from the words of the disciple Jesus loved:

> Jesus did many other miraculous signs in the presence of his disciples, which are not recorded in this book. But these are written that you may believe that Jesus is the Christ, the Son of God, and that by believing you may have life in his name. John 20:30

Closing Prayer

Lord, forgive us for the times when we behave as though we have never heard of Your resurrection. Those times when we feel hurt to the core, betrayed and in pieces, our faith in shreds. Help us now, in these precious moments, to recall the agonies You suffered in body, mind and spirit, and to accept the miracle that there is nothing we face that You do not understand.

Lift our hearts, we pray, from despair and sorrow to faith in Your promise of eternal life. Help us to worship

You as Lord of life and conqueror of death so that, held in Your love, we will not be afraid. We remember those we love and see no more, those who stand before You in ressurection light. Give us that assurance that we too will meet at the throne of grace to join the great company of saints praising You in everlasting peace and joy.

For Yours is the kingdom, the power and the glory, now and forever more. Amen.

Further Study

2 Corinthians 5:14–18; Romans 8:31–39.

The Woman Bent Double

Icebreaker

Are you a good patient? Briefly discuss the areas of incapacity you would find most difficult to cope with.

Worship Focus

Put the cross in the centre of the table, then place some pain-relief medication to one side and a hymnbook on the other.

Opening Prayer

Loving heavenly Father, as we read how Your Son healed the sick in mind, body and spirit, reveal to us the ways in which these healings were more than signs and wonders. We give thanks for modern advances in medical science, for the skill and care which have been shown to us and to those we love. Forgive us when we may have taken good health and independence for granted. Open our hearts to the miracle of life and the miracle of Your everlasting love for us. Bless us in our study, in the name of Jesus Christ, the Healer. Amen.

First Bible Reading

Luke 13:10–17

On a Sabbath Jesus was teaching in one of the synagogues, and a woman was there who had been crippled by a spirit for eighteen years. She was bent over and could not straighten up at all. When Jesus saw her, he called her forward and said to her, 'Woman, you are set free from your infirmity.' Then he put his hands on her, and immediately she straightened up and praised God.

Indignant because Jesus had healed on the Sabbath, the synagogue ruler said to the people, 'There are six days for work. So come and be healed on those days, not on the Sabbath.'

The Lord answered him, 'You hypocrites! Doesn't each

of you on the Sabbath untie his ox or donkey from the
stall and lead it out to give it water? Then should not this
woman, a daughter of Abraham, whom Satan has kept
bound for eighteen long years, be set free on the Sabbath
day from what bound her?'

When he said this, all his opponents were humiliated,
but the people were delighted with all the wonderful
things he was doing.

Setting the Scene

Jesus' teaching had covered many universally unpalatable
subjects, including: division, judgment and repentance.
Although His warnings were veiled in parables,
nevertheless, the people could not misunderstand His
meaning. Then, one Sabbath, Jesus was teaching in a
synagogue in His usual manner when He saw a woman
bent over with an unnamed disability. We need to
remember that in the synagogue the men would have
been gathered around the teacher, while the women and
children congregated at the back. If the synagogue had
been really large the women and children would have
been upstairs, but in this instance, it reads as though the
synagogue was modest and the disabled woman would
have been easily visible to Jesus from His teaching seat.

In Eugene Peterson's interpretation of the Bible, *The
Message*, he describes the woman as being twisted and
bent with arthritis. This can only be a speculative diagnosis,
but whatever it was that had crippled this poor woman for
nearly two decades, it had severely blighted her life.

This is the last time Jesus is recorded as being in a
synagogue. The Pharisees and chief priests were gathering
together all the evidence they could to incriminate Jesus
and terminate His ministry. It is obvious that the ruler of
this particular synagogue, unlike Jairus, was hostile to
Jesus of Nazareth, the healer from Galilee. But he was

too much of a coward to confront Jesus and, therefore, turned his anger on the assembled people. The woman may have been physically twisted and bent, but too many of the religious leaders were *spiritually* twisted and bent by their addiction to petty regulations. All the extra laws which had been written to augment the Ten Commandments had the effect of strangulating basic human compassion. Jesus pointed out to them that they were more concerned with the treatment of their animals than a woman in need in their own congregation. The woman hadn't expected to meet Jesus face to face, but that meeting changed her life.

Session Focus

So much of biblical teaching concerns opposites: life and death, light and dark, slave and free. This same format is found here in Luke's narrative as he enables us to observe the clash between two distinct groups of people and modes of worship. There is also the undertone of conflict between the people and the religious leaders; sickness and health, insincerity and repentance. Meeting Jesus is like a searchlight being shone into our lives – we are sharply confronted and challenged. Is our worship God-centred or is it bound up in traditions and rituals which have become the central focus? We see in Jesus' healing that God's will for us all is healing and wholeness and it is surely no coincidence that the words for 'healing' and 'salvation' are so close in the Greek language. They derive from the same root, *sozein*. Jesus comes to bring healing and salvation, He died to bring forgiveness and reconciliation between all people.

We also recognise in the hollow, self-righteous indignation of the synagogue leader how easy it is for 'correctness', political or religious, to become muddied by hypocrisy. The leader was so busy making sure everyone obeyed the rules that his heart had no room to embrace the greatest rule of all – love.

In our frighteningly technological age, there is a tendency to feel obliterated and faceless. This is such a contrary message to the one given in the life and teaching of Jesus. With the crowds of people jostling around Him, He had time for individuals like the woman trapped by her illness. The small, the weak and those unnoticed by the world are the ones chosen and loved by God.

Interlude

Song: 'Just as I am' by Charlotte Elliot
Song: 'Meekness and Majesty' by Graham Kendrick
Ave Verum by Mozart

Second Bible Reading

Luke 23:20–27

Wanting to release Jesus, Pilate appealed to them again. But they kept shouting, 'Crucify him! Crucify him!'

For the third time he spoke to them: 'Why? What crime has this man committed? I have found in him no grounds for the death penalty. Therefore I will have him punished and then release him.'

But with loud shouts they insistently demanded that he be crucified, and their shouts prevailed. So Pilate decided to grant their demand. He released the man who had been thrown into prison for insurrection and murder, the one they asked for, and surrendered Jesus to their will.

As they led him away, they seized Simon from Cyrene, who was on his way in from the country, and put the cross on him and made him carry it behind Jesus. A large number of people followed him, including women who mourned and wailed for him.

Imagine

We know from Matthew 27:55 that 'many women' had followed Jesus from Galilee to care for His needs. Imagine that the woman Jesus healed in the synagogue on a Sabbath day was one of those women. Imagine what she would have felt as she watched her Saviour dragging Himself along to Golgotha ... flogged, spat upon, tormented, insulted, bleeding, exhausted ... And imagine how you would feel watching the torture of someone you loved deeply. Imagine that you are walking beside Jesus as He staggers in the road. The soldiers push you back. You are helpless.

In these weeks of Lent, give yourself time to grasp the enormity of what happened in Jerusalem twenty centuries ago. This was God's beloved Son, bearing the hateful burden of sin, a sacrifice of love for the world ... for you and for me. Imagine Jesus' piercing gaze on our world's apathy.

Discussion Starters

1. The woman bent double was suddenly the centre of attention when Jesus called her forward. Consider her emotions as the people stared at her.

_____

_____

_____

_____

2. Have you been guilty of staring at someone's infirmity? Discuss how little provision was made in churches for people with mobility and other difficulties until European directives. Does this make you feel guilty?

_____

_____

_____

_____

3. Do you know of families where one member needs extra help? Do you just assume that the family are 'all right' or can you think of small practical ways of supporting them? What could they be?

_____

_____

_____

_____

4. When you were younger, were there things you weren't allowed to do on Sundays? How does this rate alongside the Pharisees' hypocrisy of Jesus' day? Are there things you still don't do on Sundays?

_____

_____

_____

_____

5. All Jesus' supporters seemed helpless against the power of the Sanhedrin and Pilate's decision to have Jesus crucified. In what situations today do you feel powerless and helpless?

6. Pilate was sure that Jesus was innocent, but he bowed to public opinion. In what areas do you think Christians bow to public opinion today?

7. Pilate is remembered for just one day in his life – the day when he 'washed his hands' of Jesus' death. What would you like to be remembered for?

8. 'Crowds' take on a life of their own. Discuss how quickly the behaviour of football crowds can get out of hand and the damage that otherwise responsible people can cause.

Final Thoughts

You could hardly describe two more different people than the woman bent double and the Roman governor, Pilate. One is so insignificant the Gospel author doesn't even use her name, the other is invested with the authority of Rome and has the power to let one man live and sentence another to death. Yet, their separate, brief moments face to face with Jesus have etched their memory in the minds of all who hear the Gospel stories. Such is the power in meeting Jesus. The woman was renewed. Pilate was unnerved. And what effect did meeting Jesus have on Simon, a visitor to Jerusalem forced by the soldiers to deviate from his own route? The fact that Simon is mentioned by Matthew, Mark and Luke, and that Mark names his sons, Alexander and Rufus (Mark 15:21), means we can be sure that from that day Simon's life was never the same again.

Closing Prayer

Lord Jesus, in Your compassion You touched a frail, anonymous woman.

Give us compassion, that we may strive to aid the vulnerable.

Lord Jesus, in Your teaching You exposed hypocrisy.

Give us the courage to reject pretence and insincerity.

Lord Jesus, in Your weakness a stranger carried Your burden.

Give us grace in our weakness to allow others to help us.

Lord Jesus, touch us now with forgiveness, healing and peace.

Amen.

Further Study

Matthew 5:3–12; Luke 4:16–21; Romans 16:13.

Blind Bartimaeus

Icebreaker

How many in the group are wearing glasses? What do they find most frustrating when they do not have their glasses on? Also, briefly discuss the most beautiful sights people have experienced.

Worship Focus

If you are able to borrow a book in Braille, pass it round for group members to feel – in silence – before putting it by the side of the cross on the table. On the other side of the cross place a mobile phone or a small radio.

Opening Prayer

Eternal God, open our eyes to the wonders of Your creation. Open our eyes to the blessings we hardly notice. Guide us by Your Holy Spirit to see with the eyes of faith the sacrificial love of Your Son, Jesus Christ. In the light of His love, open our eyes, our minds and our hearts to the message of salvation, the forgiveness of our sins and the promise of eternal life. We pray our prayers, spoken and unspoken, through the Spirit who strengthens us and in the name of Jesus who prays for us. Amen.

First Bible Reading
Mark 10:46–52

Then they came to Jericho. As Jesus and his disciples, together with a large crowd, were leaving the city, a blind man, Bartimaeus (that is, the Son of Timaeus), was sitting by the roadside begging. When he heard that it was Jesus of Nazareth, he began to shout, 'Jesus, Son of David, have mercy on me!'

Many rebuked him and told him to be quiet, but he shouted all the more, 'Son of David, have mercy on me!'

Jesus stopped and said, 'Call him.'

So they called to the blind man, 'Cheer up! On your

feet! He's calling you.' Throwing his cloak aside, he jumped to his feet and came to Jesus.

'What do you want me to do for you?' Jesus asked him.

The blind man said, 'Rabbi, I want to see.'

'Go,' said Jesus, 'your faith has healed you.' Immediately he received his sight and followed Jesus along the road.

Setting the Scene

Jesus was on His way to Jerusalem. The three Gospels of Matthew, Mark and Luke all record Jesus predicting His death no less than three times. Mark records Jesus' predictions in 8:31, 9:31 and 10:33–34. The triple repetition was an indication of the great importance of these statements. However, Jesus' closest disciples were so keen to avoid the subject of death that they seemed to miss the associated promise of resurrection. The state of their depression is captured in Thomas' words from John 11:16, 'Then Thomas … said to the rest of the disciples, "Let us also go, that we may die with him."'

The first time Jesus predicts His death, Peter takes his Master to one side to remonstrate with Him and to try to change His mind. This is where the phrase, 'Get thee behind me Satan' comes from. On the second occasion, the disciples were clearly unable to understand what Jesus was talking about but were afraid to ask questions. The third time it is obvious that the disciples couldn't come to terms with what Jesus was saying because James and John jump in with the totally inappropriate request to sit on either side of Jesus in glory.

In this atmosphere of gloom and apprehension, Jesus arrives in Jericho. Presumably Jesus taught in this city to great acclaim, because a large crowd gathered around Him as He and the disciples prepared to leave. It was an unusual crowd, which caught the blind beggar's attention. Again we recognise the fact that everyone was talking about Jesus of Nazareth because even the blind beggar knew who He was. Suddenly, filled with hope that this healing rabbi might help him, he begins to yell for Jesus. Compare his shouts with words from the prophet Jeremiah, '"The days are coming," declares the LORD, "when I will raise up to David a righteous Branch, a King who will reign wisely and do what is just and right in the land"' (Jer. 23:5). Also, look at Ezekiel 37:24–25. Deeply rooted in their Scripture, and therefore in the hearts and minds of the nation, was God's promise that their Saviour would come from the royal line of King David. To call a man 'Son of David' was the greatest accolade and one which was used again for Jesus when He entered Jerusalem on what we now call Palm Sunday: 'Blessed is the coming kingdom of our father David!' (Mark 11:10). This Davidic line was also specified by the Gospel writers Luke (2:4) and Matthew (1:6). When reading these stories about Jesus we need to hold in our minds the fact that the Jews were an occupied nation and there were repeated insurgencies which the Romans squashed (Luke 23:19). A blind man, known only by his father's name, unable to work, useless to his family and community, relegated to the gutter, cries out to meet Jesus.

Session Focus

In the words of the late Rev Dr Donald English, 'in Mark's gospel it is the response of faith commitment which provides the arena within which the drama of salvation takes place'. Take into account the life of rejection this beggar was living. In those days blindness was considered a curse from God and so this man was viewed as a non-person. We may not know his name, but we can be in no doubt about his desperation to be healed, his persistence and his total faith in Jesus.

This passage also sheds light on the crowd that was following Jesus through Jericho. The 'Law' which the

Pharisees and Temple priests were so quick to turn against Jesus, also made provision for people such as blind Bartimaeus: 'If one of your countrymen becomes poor and is unable to support himself among you, help him as you would an alien or a temporary resident …' (Lev. 25:35). In contrast to this rule of kindness, and reminiscent of the disciples shooing away the children, it seems that the crowd just left the beggar in the dust. The only notice they took of the man was to tell him, in terse Aramaic, to 'shut up!' These were people on the way to Jerusalem to celebrate the Feast of Passover! Let us never forget that our reaction to those around us speaks louder than words.

Jesus hears the cries and stops. He takes time to meet the beggar. Jesus released him from the prison of his blindness. There was no need to beg anymore, no more living a shunned existence, not knowing when he woke whether he would eat that day. Jesus gave him back his worth and independence, and the man's response was to immediately become a follower. His liberation enabled him to follow Jesus along the road … to Jerusalem.

Interlude

Hymn: 'Amazing Grace' by John Newton
Song: 'Jesus, you are changing me' by (blind musician) Marilyn Baker
Part of *Sonata Pathetique* by Beethoven

Second Bible Reading

Mark 15:22–32
They brought Jesus to the place called Golgotha (which means The Place of the Skull). Then they offered him wine mixed with myrrh, but he did not take it. And they crucified him. Dividing up his clothes, they cast lots to see what each would get.

It was the third hour when they crucified him. The written notice of the charge against him read: THE KING OF THE JEWS. They crucified two robbers with him, one on his right and one on his left. Those who passed by hurled insults at him, shaking their heads and saying, 'So! You who are going to destroy the temple and build it in three days, come down from the cross and save yourself!'

In the same way the chief priests and the teachers of the law mocked him among themselves. 'He saved others,' they said, 'but he can't save himself! Let this Christ, this King of Israel, come down now from the cross, that we may see and believe.' Those crucified with him also heaped insults on him.

Imagine

Imagine Bartimaeus delighting in all the colours and shapes and sights of Jerusalem. He can't stop praising God for the miracle Jesus performed in his life. He can see his family, he can see Jesus, he can see the City of David and the dominating glory of the Temple. Imagine his distress when he sees Jesus nailed to a cross and wrenched into position between two thieves … The soldiers were murdering his Saviour. Could he bear to watch or did he hide his eyes in misery and despair?

And take yourself to that place called Golgotha. Imagine you are standing behind the women near the cross. You hear the strangled words from Jesus, 'Father, forgive them for they do not know what they are doing.' Then imagine you hear the final shout: 'It is finished.' How would you respond?

Discussion Starters

1. The blind man was known by his father's name. Discuss how many people you think of in relation to someone else? For example: Jack's wife, or Helen's boss.

_____
_____
_____
_____

2. The son of Timaeus made sure he didn't lose his chance of meeting Jesus by shouting to Him. Have you ever been told to keep quiet when you wanted to speak?

_____
_____
_____
_____

3. When Jesus called, Bartimaeus rushed to His side. If Jesus called you, would you rush to be with Him or would there be some things you would need to attend to first?

_____
_____
_____
_____

4. Often people show a great hesitation to talk about 'faith'. Do you feel embarrassed when you are asked about your faith? In what situations is it easiest to discuss matters of faith?

_____
_____
_____
_____

5. What would be your request of Jesus?

_____

_____

_____

_____

6. Crowds of people watched crucifixions. Hundreds watched public hangings. Today, films and video games offer brutality as 'entertainment'. What is our Christian response?

_____

_____

_____

_____

7. How do we respond to suffering in the world – for example, the suffering we see in places like Darfur, Zimbabwe and Gaza?

_____

_____

_____

_____

8. Discuss the symbolism of the robbers hanging on each side of Jesus in the context of His teaching about the King separating the sheep from the goats (Matt. 25:31–46).

_____

_____

_____

_____

Final Thoughts

The sight of a beggar, whether in Europe, the Middle East or on the continents of South America, Africa or India, is always uncomfortable. We tend to want to avert our gaze, but Jesus did the opposite. He stopped for, called to and gazed on Bartimaeus. With regard to the other crucified prisoners: we often don't have much time for prisoners, but Jesus used His last gasps to reassure the repentant thief. Jesus gave His time and effort to the people society despised and wished to forget. As His followers, this too is our challenge and our mission in His name.

Closing Prayer

(Leader to read. All: Responses in bold.)

For giving us the freedom to choose between good and evil,
the freedom to respond to you in thanks and love,
Loving God: **We thank you.**

For sending your Son, Jesus Christ,
who, by dying on the cross,
revealed the depth of your forgiving love for us,
Loving God: **We thank you**.

As we remember the death of Jesus,
our hearts are full of gratitude for such a love
freely given,
not counting the cost,
poured out for all.
Saving God, we praise and thank you.[1]

Further Study

The Book of Wisdom 4:7–15 (Apocrypha); Isaiah 53:1–12.

Note

1. Donald Hilton (ed.), *Seasons and Celebrations* (NCEC, 1996). Selected verses of prayer by Christine Odell from p.123. Used by permission.

Nicodemus and Joseph of Arimathea

Icebreaker

Do you have interests or hobbies of which most people are unaware? See how many different interests are represented in the group.

Worship Focus

Place a bowl of pot pouri beside the cross, together with some strips of linen to represent the linen strips wrapped around Jesus' body at His burial.

Opening Prayer

LEADER: Lord Jesus, as we come to the last in our current studies together, we pray for the touch of Your Holy Spirit on all we have shared.

ALL: We commit ourselves to follow You, because You are the Way. We commit ourselves to believe in You, because You are the Truth. We commit all we are and, in Your love may become, into Your eternal keeping, because You are the Life. We worship You in spirit and in truth, our Lord and our God. Amen.

First Bible Reading

John 19:38–42

Later, Joseph of Arimathea asked Pilate for the body of Jesus. Now Joseph was a disciple of Jesus, but secretly because he feared the Jews. With Pilate's permission, he came and took the body away. He was accompanied by Nicodemus, the man who earlier had visited Jesus by night. Nicodemus brought a mixture of myrrh and aloes, about seventy-five pounds. Taking Jesus' body, the two of them wrapped it, with the spices, in strips of linen. This was in accordance with Jewish burial customs. At the place where Jesus was crucified, there was a garden, and in the garden a new tomb, in which no-one had ever been laid. Because it was the Jewish day of

Preparation and since the tomb was near by, they laid Jesus there.

Setting the Scene

The 'show' was over. The crowd had melted away. The curious, the abusive, the distraught; men and women, soldiers … all gone their separate ways. There was nothing more to see, Jesus had not saved Himself, there had been no last fantastic miracle … Jesus was dead.

Jesus died at about three o'clock on the afternoon before the Sabbath. The Jewish Sabbath was our Saturday, so we can fix Jesus' death on Friday – a Friday forever in the calendar as Good Friday or Sad Friday. 'Good' because Jesus died to take away the sins of the world and therefore Christians can rejoice at their salvation; 'Sad' (in some Eastern European countries) because of the divine tragedy.

The disciples were terrified for their own lives, emotionally devastated by the overwhelming awfulness of the crucifixion and, to compound their problems, they were outsiders from Galilee, unfamiliar with what their options now were. Joseph and Nicodemus were Pharisees of Jerusalem; they had status, knowledge and connections, and they realised that, because of the Sabbath, they had to act quickly. There was very little time for the men to approach Pilate, then return to Golgotha for the body and complete their act of love before sunset, when the Sabbath began.

The women who had stood vigil at the foot of the cross were paralysed with grief yet they must have been so relieved by the quick actions of these two Pharisees. In a poignant sentence, Matthew records: 'Mary Magdalene and the other Mary were sitting there opposite the tomb' (Matt. 27:61). They witnessed the ritual burial. They could do nothing, but at least they could report the reverent burial to Jesus' mother and His disciples.

Jesus had taught, 'many who are first will be last, and the last first' (Mark 10:31), and there, in those sombre moments, the teaching found an ironic truth. The two Pharisees, members of the Jewish court, the Sanhedrin, who had held back in their public support for Jesus of Nazareth, were the last people to be considered disciples. But, it was these two men who came into the open to administer orthodox burial rites to their dead Lord.

Session Focus

What an incredible and highly public change had come over Nicodemus and his fellow member of the Sanhedrin, Joseph of Arimathea! They may have been admirers of Jesus, but they had kept the fact a close secret until this dramatic change of heart. Remember, Nicodemus was the Pharisee who had visited Jesus under cover of darkness (John 3:1–21). And maybe it was Nicodemus, together with Joseph, who were the 'some Pharisees' who, according to Luke 13:31, went to Jesus and warned Him to leave Jerusalem.

Both had remained silent, or were diplomatically absent, when Jesus was taken before the Sanhedrin but, when they saw Jesus die, they became brave enough to go to Pilate to ask for the release of Jesus' body for burial. Traditionally, traitors would have been left hanging as an example and other criminals were tossed into a communal grave. Clearly Pilate placed Jesus in neither of these categories. By releasing the body for private burial, Pilate gave a further sign that he found Jesus to be an innocent victim.

Jesus, who had been crucified with the notice above His head, 'THE KING OF THE JEWS', received a royal burial from Nicodemus and Joseph. Nicodemus brought a vast quantity of spices and they tenderly laid the bloodied, lifeless body of their Lord in clean linen in Joseph's personal new tomb. Their silence was over. Their secret admiration now a public display of love and honour. Their fear was supplanted by their need to redress their previous timidity and shame. They gave their dead Jesus the best they had to offer.

Interlude

Hymn: 'When I survey the wondrous cross' by Isaac Watts
Hymn: 'There is a green hill far away' by C.F. Alexander
Lacrimosa Requiem by Mozart
'Pie Jesu' from *Requiem* by Andrew Lloyd Webber

Second Bible Reading

Matthew 27:59–66

Joseph took the body, wrapped it in a clean linen cloth, and placed it in his own new tomb that he had cut out of the rock. He rolled a big stone in front of the entrance to the tomb and went away. Mary Magdalene and the other Mary were sitting there opposite the tomb.

The next day, the one after the Preparation Day, the chief priests and the Pharisees went to Pilate. 'Sir,' they said, 'we remember that while he was still alive that deceiver said, "After three days I will rise again." So give the order for the tomb to be made secure until the third day. Otherwise, his disciples may come and steal the body and tell the people that he has been raised from the dead. This last deception will be worse than the first.'

'Take a guard,' Pilate answered. 'Go, make the tomb as secure as you know how.' So they went and made the tomb secure by putting a seal on the stone and posting the guard.

Imagine

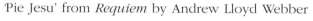

If Joseph and Nicodemus had been present when Jesus was brought before Caiaphas and the Sanhedrin, imagine how compromised they would have felt. As the

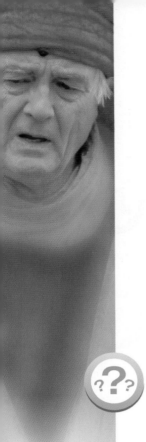

false witnesses came and testified against Jesus, how disillusioned they must have been. Do you imagine that they could meet Jesus' steady gaze as He stood silently before them? They knew this 'trial' was illegal and, knowing the Sanhedrin had no authority to pass a death sentence, they were probably praying that Jesus would just be whipped before being banished back to Galilee. Think of them turning the predicament over and over in their minds: even if Jesus was sent to Pilate, the Governor wouldn't be bothered with a Galilean preacher. He had far more dangerous criminals in his dungeons. Imagine their horror when they discovered that Pilate had bowed to public pressure and Jesus was going to be crucified.

If you had been part of that Sanhedrin, do you imagine you would have been strong enough to speak up for Jesus?

Discussion Starters

1. How would you feel as the wife of either Nicodemus or Joseph when you knew by burying Jesus' body they were acting against the chief priest, Caiaphas?

2. Compare the sealing of the tomb to Daniel 6:16–23.

3. The religious leaders' obsession to have Jesus killed led them to pervert the justice they were appointed to protect. Discuss ways in which obsessions can become dangerous.

_____

_____

_____

_____

4. The chief priests and Pharisees remembered Jesus' prophecy that He would be raised from the dead on the third day (Matt. 20:17–19). They remembered and were afraid. What teaching of Jesus do you remember which gives you hope and comfort?

_____

_____

_____

_____

5. The stone in front of the tomb would have been like an enormous circular millstone. Think about any large 'barriers' that are keeping you from Jesus.

_____

_____

_____

_____

6. What do you think the disciples' opinion of Nicodemus and Joseph of Arimathea would have been?

_____

_____

_____

_____

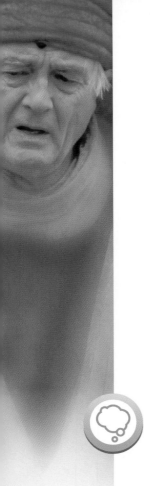

7. There are three 'gardens' mentioned in the Bible. The Garden of Eden, the Garden of Gethsemane and the garden where Joseph of Arimathea had his tomb. Look at the contrasts between these 'gardens'.

_____

_____

_____

_____

8. Jesus died on the cross in our place. It was not a faked death but an agonising human death, a death prophesised both in Scripture and by Jesus Himself. God did this for you – how do you want to respond?

_____

_____

_____

_____

Final Thoughts

The great prophet, Isaiah, uttered words from God, 'For my thoughts are not your thoughts, neither are your ways my ways ...' (Isa. 55:8). The Jews were longing for a leader, a Messiah who would free them from Roman rule. They wanted to see power and might, and probably a good dash of vengeance as well. They were unprepared for the Messiah who came to bring victory over sin and death and whose teaching called for a revolution within their own hearts. They couldn't understand a Saviour of the lost and marginalised, the small and vulnerable.

How similar it is for us today. We are too prone to acknowledge wealth, power and influence while the kingdom of justice and peace, the forgiveness of sins and the life everlasting is put on the back burner. Let us realise the truth that God's ways are not the ways of the world. And through this study, through meeting Jesus, may our lives, like the lives of the people we have studied, be transfigured by His love.

Closing Prayer

LEADER: As we end our Lent study, we thank You, Lord Jesus, that there is no end to Your living presence with us. Guide us by Your Holy Spirit to radiate Your peace and compassion to all.

So now may God the Father encourage us, Jesus our Saviour renew us and the gift of the Holy Spirit transform us.

You may like to join together in the Grace, found at the end of Paul's second letter to the Christians in Corinth, 2 Corinthians 13:14:

May the grace of the Lord Jesus Christ, and the love of God, and the fellowship of the Holy Spirit be with [us] all.
Amen.

Further Study:

Psalm 38:7–12; Romans 5:1–11.

THIS IS NOT THE LAST PAGE!

Grace and peace to you from him who is, and who was, and who is to come … and from Jesus Christ, who is the faithful witness, the firstborn from the dead, and the ruler of the kings of the earth.

To him who loves us and has freed us from our sins by his blood … to him be glory and power for ever and ever! Amen.

Revelation 1:4–6

The next page to be written is *your* page in the Book of Life. Your continuing pilgrimage in prayer, words, actions, faith, hope and love …

THIS IS NOT THE END.

THANKS BE TO GOD!

Leader's Notes

These notes are designed as an aid to group leaders, especially if you have not led a group before.

Suggestions on Using this Book

Each study is designed to last a minimum of sixty minutes and a maximum of ninety minutes. (Timings for the different sections in each study are suggested below.)

Icebreaker (eight to ten minutes)

Most likely a minute each will be more than enough for members of the group to share something. This section also allows a small space for anyone who is unavoidably late to join the session without missing the worship.

Worship Focus and Opening Prayer (five minutes)

Ideally, find a small table, cover with a purple cloth and place on it a free-standing cross at the centre back. Choose whether the symbols suggested for the session are already in place as people arrive or whether it is more significant to place them during the Worship Focus. You may wish to include the Lord's Prayer with the Opening Prayers. It is helpful to use the word 'Amen', as it makes a fitting close to prayer time.

Bible Readings (three to four minutes' each)

Try to avoid asking someone to read with fifteen seconds' notice. Ask the person at the end of the previous session if they would like to read at the following meeting. Not everyone in the group will be confident with reading in public.

Setting the Scene and Session Focus (five minutes)

These sections could be read by different group members.

Interlude (two to four minutes)

This gives a linking pause between the readings and you

will be surprised how much music can be heard in two minutes. Most hymns are about four minutes' long. You will need to select which music to use before each session.

Imagine (two minutes)

After meeting Jesus, our seven characters' lives continued. We 'imagine' how they might have felt hearing and seeing what happened to Jesus in that week before Passover in Jerusalem. Thinking about them like this helps us realise that they were actual people whose lives were never the same again. Then we 'imagine' how we would feel seeing and hearing those same things. How do we respond?

Discussion Starters (twenty-five minutes)

You need to use discretion and allow more time here if the session is to be ninety minutes' long.

Final Thoughts (two minutes)

This section is best read by the leader to focus the group's thoughts on the truths revealed from the study. If ninety minutes have been allowed for the session, you may like to ask if anyone has a further insight to add.

Closing Prayer (three to four minutes)

You may feel that current local, national or international events may need to be included in this time of prayer. The group may also like to conclude by saying The Grace together in blessing one another.

Further Study

If members of the group would like to continue their reflections throughout the week, these sections offer relevant Bible references.

General Comments

It is important for the leader to read each week's study well beforehand and to decide how best the material will work with the group. For instance, the suggested hymns and music under the heading 'Interlude' need to be sourced so that CDs, tapes, a pianist, hymnbooks, etc are ready and waiting. As the leader, you may choose to begin the Worship Focus by asking everyone to sing together one of the hymns and then use the Interlude time for the 'listening' music. It will all depend on your group and the members' readiness to sing – and the numbers. It would not be kind to insist on three members singing, unaccompanied, all the verses of 'The Servant King' – they may not attend again! In all areas there is a need to know and be sensitive to your group, so that they will feel comfortable, and all may be enriched in a spirit of trust.

Some leaders may find it best to pose one of the Discussion Starters earlier in the session, perhaps directly following the Bible reading. And do not feel compelled to plough through all eight questions. Remember they are Discussion *Starters* and sometimes other questions will flow from what the group shares. Be open to allow people to share issues which concern them, but also be ready to move on if somebody begins to take over discussion.

At the end of the first session, encourage different people to read the Opening Prayer and Closing Prayer sections next time, so there are separate voices reading. You could also ask someone to read the Bible portions and another to read the Imagine section. This has a dual advantage in that people will feel valued and included and also changes in pace and voice help to maintain concentration and stimulate interest.

Don't forget to thank the group for getting together and taking part. If applicable, thank the person who hosts the session. And don't let the sessions over-run. If possible, sit where you can see a clock so that you keep a check on how the session is progressing without people thinking (or seeing) you are looking at your watch!

Prayer is essential. The leader is the enabler and the leader is enabled only by the Holy Spirit. Jesus said: '... the Holy Spirit, whom the Father will send in my name, will teach you all things and will remind you of everything I have said to you' (John 14:26).

National Distributors

UK: (and countries not listed below)
CWR, Waverley Abbey House, Waverley Lane, Farnham, Surrey GU9 8EP.
Tel: (01252) 784700 Outside UK (44) 1252 784700

AUSTRALIA: CMC Australasia, PO Box 519, Belmont, Victoria 3216.
Tel: (03) 5241 3288 Fax: (03) 5241 3290

CANADA: Cook Communications Ministries, PO Box 98, 55 Woodslee Avenue, Paris, Ontario N3L 3E5.
Tel: 1800 263 2664

GHANA: Challenge Enterprises of Ghana, PO Box 5723, Accra.
Tel: (021) 222437/223249 Fax: (021) 226227

HONG KONG: Cross Communications Ltd, 1/F, 562A Nathan Road, Kowloon.
Tel: 2780 1188 Fax: 2770 6229

INDIA: Crystal Communications, 10-3-18/4/1, East Marredpalli, Secunderabad – 500026, Andhra
Pradesh. Tel/Fax: (040) 27737145

KENYA: Keswick Books and Gifts Ltd, PO Box 10242, Nairobi.
Tel: (02) 331692/226047 Fax: (02) 728557

MALAYSIA: Salvation Book Centre (M) Sdn Bhd, 23 Jalan SS 2/64, 47300 Petaling Jaya, Selangor.
Tel: (03) 78766411/78766797 Fax: (03) 78757066/78756360

NEW ZEALAND: CMC Australasia, PO Box 303298, North Harbour, Auckland 0751.
Tel: 0800 449 408 Fax: 0800 449 049

NIGERIA: FBFM, Helen Baugh House, 96 St Finbarr's College Road, Akoka, Lagos.
Tel: (01) 7747429/4700218/825775/827264

PHILIPPINES: OMF Literature Inc, 776 Boni Avenue, Mandaluyong City.
Tel: (02) 531 2183 Fax: (02) 531 1960

SINGAPORE: Alby Commercial Enterprises Pte Ltd, 95 Kallang Avenue #04-00, AIS Industrial Building,
339420. Tel: (65) 629 27238 Fax: (65) 629 27235

SOUTH AFRICA: Struik Christian Books, 80 MacKenzie Street, PO Box 1144, Cape Town 8000.
Tel: (021) 462 4360 Fax: (021) 461 3612

SRI LANKA: Christombu Publications (Pvt) Ltd, Bartleet House, 65 Braybrooke Place, Colombo 2.
Tel: (9411) 2421073/2447665

TANZANIA: CLC Christian Book Centre, PO Box 1384, Mkwepu Street, Dar es Salaam.
Tel/Fax: (022) 2119439

USA: Cook Communications Ministries, PO Box 98, 55 Woodslee Avenue, Paris, Ontario N3L 3E5,
Canada. Tel: 1800 263 2664

ZIMBABWE: Word of Life Books (Pvt) Ltd, Christian Media Centre, 8 Aberdeen Road, Avondale, PO Box
A480 Avondale, Harare. Tel: (04) 333355 or 091301188

For email addresses, visit the CWR website: www.cwr.org.uk
CWR is a Registered Charity – Number 294387
CWR is a Limited Company registered in England – Registration Number 1990308

Day and Residential Courses
Counselling Training
Leadership Development
Biblical Study Courses
Regional Seminars
Ministry to Women
Daily Devotionals
Books and Videos
Conference Centre

Trusted all Over the World

CWR HAS GAINED A WORLDWIDE reputation as a centre of excellence for Bible-based training and resources. From our headquarters at Waverley Abbey House, Farnham, England, we have been serving God's people for 40 years with a vision to help apply God's Word to everyday life and relationships. The daily devotional *Every Day with Jesus* is read by nearly a million readers an issue in more than 150 countries, and our unique courses in biblical studies and pastoral care are respected all over the world. Waverley Abbey House provides a conference centre in a tranquil setting.

For free brochures on our seminars and courses, conference facilities, or a catalogue of CWR resources, please contact us at the following address.
CWR, Waverley Abbey House, Waverley Lane, Farnham, Surrey GU9 8EP, UK

Telephone: **+44 (0)1252 784700**
Email: **mail@cwr.org.uk**
Website: **www.cwr.org.uk**

 CWR Applying God's Word
to everyday life and relationships

Cover to Cover Complete

Packed into this single volume is everything you need for a thrilling chronological voyage of discovery through the whole Bible as it happened. Based on the original acclaimed reading plan, *Cover to Cover,* this complete volume includes:

- charts, maps, illustrations and diagrams
- a timeline on every page
- devotional thoughts for contemplation each day
- and – for the first time – the complete Bible text.

There is also a related website featuring character studies, readers' testimonies, helpful hints and much more.

£19.99
Special introductory offer: £17.99 (until 31 December 2007)
ISBN: 978-1-85345-433-2

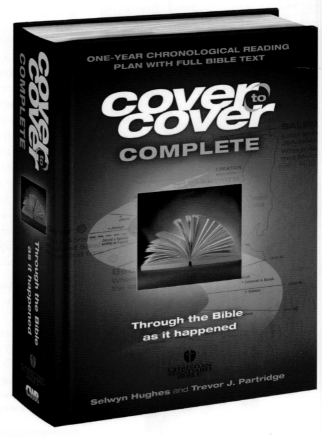

ONE-YEAR CHRONOLOGICAL READING PLAN WITH FULL BIBLE TEXT

cover to cover

COMPLETE

Through the Bible as it happened

Selwyn Hughes and Trevor J. Partridge

Prices correct at time of printing.